A Bouquet

Of

Poems

Leeza Wilson

A Bouquet of Poems ©2017 by Leeza Wilson

All rights reserved. No part of this book may be used or reproduced or transmitted in any form or by any means, electronic or mechanical, including photocopying, recording, or by any information storage and retrieval system, without written permission by the author except in the case of brief quotations embodied in critical articles or reviews.

Edited and Published by Tsarina Press

ISBN 978-1-948429-08-5

Dedication

This book is dedicated in loving memory of my dad, David. He inspired my love of reading and writing. His poetry inspired me to try writing it. At the end of this book I have included the few poems he wrote that my mom and I were able to preserve. With love to a great man who is dearly missed.

March 27, 1936 to March 1, 2017

Table of Contents

Spring	1
The Willow	2
My Weeping Willow	3
The Pecan Tree	4
Storm Rising	4
Autumn Dawn	6
My Russia	7
The Land of Rus	8
Inspiration	9
The Game	9
Solitary	10
Dear Time	10
Denied	11
The Cycle of Life	11
A Riddle	12
Who Am I?	13
Mother	14
Music Within Me	15
Worthless Words	16
I Choose	17
The Man of Darkness	18
Where Does Justice Live	20
Don't Laugh At Me	21
The Broken Brotherhood	22
Stalin	23
The Skater	24

Attraction	25
Longing	26
Loneliness	26
Betrayal	27
Sorrow	27
Black Heart	28
Skeletons	29
Missing	29
Mine	30
Hearts in Clouds	31
My Love	31
Without You	32
Valeriy	32
My Slava	33
Poems by My Dad	35
God	37
Sympathy	37
Love	38
Time	39
Life	40
Love Always	41
A Dream	41
My Love	42
Eternity	43
Just Me and My Grandson	44

A Bouquet Of Poems

Spring

Spring has sprung
A new world begun
Of rabbits hopping
And of flowers the rainbow popping
The trees are budding
The children running

In its warmth the sun embraces me
Enchanted I am by the singing bees
Fairies and sailboats in the skies
Drift by with whispering sighs

Leeza Wilson

The Willow

The willow,
Cool and shady
Are your embracing limbs.
They shield me from
The ball of fire
High in the sky.
In the cooling breeze
Your talent is seen
As your sinewy limbs
Gracefully dance in the wind

My Weeping Willow

My weeping willow is a safe haven,
A hiding place from fears and troubles.
Under its drooping branches
Its feathery leaves conceal me from the world.
To another land I'm whisked away upon entering its dome
Where my childhood memories roam.
For inspiration it is my home.
My weeping willow cries in the rain.
Its tears wash away my pain.
When the sun is beating down
I feel not a ray.
My weeping willow shades me all day.
With a gentle breeze its boughs dance
In such a mesmerizing way.
And on a cold wintry day
It holds me in a warm embrace.
My beautiful weeping willow.

The Pecan Tree

Stretching into the heavens
Reaching out with its strong branches
Fluffed with leaves the yard it shades
And shields the swing from the sun's rays
The back porch it cools with wispy breezes
When the autumn comes, its fruit it rains
Covering the ground in a blanket of pecans
With glee we gather the loot
Filling pails to carry us the year through

Storm Rising

Jangling wind chimes tickling my ears.
Rumbling tin roof arousing my dog's fears.
Rustling leaves through bending boughs.
Darkening clouds floating on the winds.
Blinding lightening piercing the graying skies.
Deafening thunder pealing as heaven cries.

Leeza Wilson

Autumn Dawn

Twinkling lights
Brightening the night
Flying by like
Shooting stars
Frost fading
On the windscreen
Emerging dawn veiling
The heavenly stars
Fog lifting from the
Crystal covered field
Daystar rising
Across the dawning sky
Through a shroud of fog
Peaks the mountain high
Over the rolling hills

My Russia

Rugged mountains dividing the realms
Tops covered in glistening snow
Under a thick gray sky the wild roams
Birches and brush blanketed in snow
Bright onion domes reaching into the heavens
Artic foxes peaking from their dens
A glint of sun through parting clouds
Icicles shimmering under the sun's rays
Colorful dachas painting the lands
Troikas racing through the snows
A masterpiece made by God's own hands

The Land of Rus

Vast white expanse extends
As far as the eye can see.
Our troika speeds past the birch forest as
Small wooden dachas rise across the land,
Splashing color onto a pallet of white
With their bright facades
And window frames of intricate design.
In our troika we speed along.
A church appears on the horizon.
Its tall spires reach high into the sky.
Against the white snow and gray sky
Its cupolas glisten as a hint of sun peaks out.
The clouds thicken and again the snow falls.
In the distance another troika passes by.
The howling winds bring heavier snows
Laying a blanket for the night.
We park the troika and barn the horses.
Nothing more stirs as dusk descends
On this cold wintry night.
All are snuggled warmly in their dens.

Inspiration

For a writer inspiration is a must
For without it the mind will rust
And the heart and soul will bust
Then the writer will just
Become an empty, bitter crust

The Game

The music plays hypnotically.
The bright colors draw the player in,
Gluing his eyes to the screen.
The story engages him.
Can it do any harm
That he's capture by its charm?
But why all the alarm?
After all, it's only a game.
So what if he's hooked from
Dawn to dusk and dusk to dawn.
Relentlessly he plays.
Is the player playing the game,
Or the game playing the player?

Leeza Wilson

Solitary

Small window in steel door
On four gray walls opens forth
Dirty grey floors
Tiny window with steel bars
By one wall a lumpy cot
With covers folded on top
In corner is a stainless steel sink
And a pot nearby with a stink
Musty odor throughout
One dimly lit bulb
Soon to burn out

Dear Time

Oh dear time,
Please allow me
These few lines
Just this one time
For to me
These lines are
Not just a rhyme
But they are my lifeline

Denied

I ask to be allowed through the gate.
But you say, "No.
Our decision is not based on hate.
However, for you trust will come late."
You base your decision on ones I do not know.
Through your blockade
My abilities I cannot show.
So if you will please,
Remove the scales of prejudice from your eyes
You will be pleasantly surprised.

The Cycle of Life

Life is known for its unexpected turns.
As a cyclone it churns.
And our hopes and dreams it flings
As if they are nothing.
Our hearts for true love yearn.
But by false, deceptive love they are burned.
For justice our spirits cry out.
But does anyone hear us shout?
Our minds and souls are completely worn out
As our trust is powdered into dust.

Leeza Wilson

A Riddle

What do you hear
With your inner ear
When lines and rhymes
Of poetry dance and prance
While night becomes light?

Does the fright
To not be able to write
Leave you quaking in fear at night
That what you hear
With your inner ear
No one else ever will?

Who Am I?

Who am I?
I am the tree in the forest that fell
When no one was near to hear.
Who am I?
I am a mouse in a trap
That everyone views as crap.
Who am I?
I am a warped board
That everyone sees as useless.
Who am I?
I am the kid in the hall
Who is bullied by all.
Who are you?

Leeza Wilson

Mother

Maid for everyone at home.
Overworked beyond belief.
Tired all the time.
Heavy heart from the burden carried
Every day the same as before.
Ready for relief.

Music Within Me

Music is the essence of my soul.
Its beat is the pulse that drives
The rhythm of my life.
The melody is the blood
That courses through my veins.
A world without music would be
Like a world without air.
Music is my soul.
It invigorates my spirit.
The harmonies carry me
As if on wings of eagles
Through peaceful skies
Soaring to unreachable heights.

Leeza Wilson

Worthless Words

Why do the meaningful and inspired words
Always come when I lay down
My weary head to sleep;
When the heavy weight of fatigue
Presses down on me,
Chaining me to my bed so helplessly?
While in my head eloquent words
Tumble around fluidly into beautiful phrases,
My spirit alone is able to rise.
To my desk it goes
For my pen and pad.
My body is willing to rise,
But my bed reaches out and
Its arms hold me to the mattress,
Leaving my inspired words
To dangle in the air.
Those words never again to be recreated
In such sweet perfection.
They fade away into the deep trance of sleep,
Making them worthless words longing for a pen and pad.

I Choose

I choose to dwell in the essence of reprieve
And to alter my choice upon my mood.
I choose today
To remember the error of my ways,
But tomorrow that choice may be forgotten.
I choose to accept my fortune,
Or my lack thereof,
For God has promised us nothing
But what we need.
I choose to strive toward understanding
The ways of man,
Especially those that prove elusive.
I choose to embrace those things
Which I cannot change,
And for those that I can change,
I cherish for their flexibility.
I choose to enjoy the rights
That I am freely given,
And do not long for those
That I am not meant to have.
I choose not to wallow in self-pity, but rather
To gather up the broken pieces of tragedy
And mold them
Into an honorable new creation.
I choose to look forward to the future
With hope, and view the past
As a necessary evil for personal growth.

Leeza Wilson

The Man of Darkness

Man of Darkness appearing as Angel of Light.
His vehicle—the pale horse of the Apocalypse.
His home—a web of deception
From which his false light gleams.
In the shadows hides his spiral staircase of lies
Climbing clear up to the skies.
He stands shrouded
Behind a curtain of holiness
So sheer it barely exists.
The persistent boil from private,
Forbidden pleasures brands his masculinity.
His dark hair, eyes, and skin the only
Visual perception seen by the holy
Of the darkness hidden within.
His forked tongue hypnotizes
The Men of Justice
And glazes their eyes over
With the scales of the serpent.
With melodious words as soothing as
The snake charmer's tune
He lulls the innocent into a euphoria of belief,
And in their dull stupor
He squeezes out their senses
With his stifling tendrils of
Unadorned repentance.

Meanwhile, his father the Serpent
Looks on with an approving smile.
Praising the Man of Darkness,
The Serpent says,
"Job well done, My Son!"

Leeza Wilson

Where Does Justice Live

Where does justice live?
For within the boundaries of earth
It does not reside.
Far off from us humans justice is hid.
Its very essence is unreachably high.
Into the clouds and fog of hatred and malice our plea is bid,
Only to be denied.

Tears of pain and anguish pour like rain.
But the anguish of heart is deemed a fib.
Still searching for justice with eyes strained,
Our bleeding souls trudge on tired and ripped.
Impatiently we wait for injustice to be brought to shame,
While evil rules and oppresses us with fists,
Forcing the innocent to wear the blame.
Where does justice live?

Don't Laugh At Me

Please don't laugh at me.
For you know not who I am.
You know not who I was,
And you know not who I can be.
So please don't laugh at me.
A wounded soldier is still a soldier.
A fallen hero is still a hero.
A disabled person is still a person.
Please don't laugh at me.
Our imperfections do not change
Our mind and heart
But they can bruise the soul
And break the spirit.
So please don't laugh at me.
Given the chance to live free,
I can show you just who I can be.
But please don't laugh at me.

Leeza Wilson

The Broken Brotherhood

Standing in the middle of the crowd,
But on the outside looking in.
Faint laughter and conversation coming
From the circle I stand within.
Their fault-finding eyes and whispers
Pierce through my soul.
Like icy daggers, they fill me with holes.
When the flames roar and we're in the heat
There is no love and loyalty to me.
Their strength from me they hold back.
Support for me they lack.
In the heat of the flames
They should have my back,
But to them I am nothing
And fall through the crack.

Stalin

Cold was his heart
As in history he played his part
Calculating was his ways
All throughout his days
Ruthless was the punishment
As firm and set as cement
Easily his anger would blaze
With hate his eyes would haze
No one was safe
Under his realm of hate
To the gulag people would go
And their whereabouts no one would know
His inner circle before him would stare
Feeling secure they laid their hearts bare
Standing under the red star
Striving to reach the bar
But cold was his heart
And for justice there was no part

Leeza Wilson

The Skater

Standing with the poise of a ballerina
Movements graceful and flowing
With a firm, taut body
Soft, delicate features
And gracious, humble smile
Eyes sparkling with delight
Each skating element completed
A flawless performance
A beauty on ice
A joyful heart
A gracious crowd

Attraction

The days seem shorter
The evenings feel longer
The sun feels warmer
The nights feel cooler

Your embrace soothes me
Your words amuse me
Your touch excites me
Your smile pleases me

How wonderful that
Such a man exists
How remarkable
That you chose me
To share your hot river
Of passionate love

Longing

I hear your voice calling to me,
Though distant it seems to be.
And yet it calls to me so clearly
As if you were standing before me.
But I see you not
And I know not to where you've got.
Your lips I still taste,
And my heart beats with haste.
Your hot breath on my skin I can feel
As if your presence was real.

Loneliness

Yet again I crawl into my lonely bed,
And stare at the empty spot beside me.
I long for the man who should be there.
But who is he? Where is he?
Will I ever find him?
How will I ever find him?
My heart breaks and sorrow pours forth.
Tears of loneliness trickle down my cheeks
As I drift into an unhappy sleep.

Betrayal

Your envious green eyes
Slice right through me
By your lustful greed
For lascivious pleasures.
My bleeding soul laid bare
My shattered heart trampled upon
So carelessly as if by a dare
My trust in shreds
And you don't even care

Sorrow

Aching heart
Joy snuffed out
Dreams shattered
Future perished
You are my one true regret

Leeza Wilson

Black Heart

My black heart
Stabbed to death
By your love
Squeezed and bled dry
By your suffocating tendrils
No more desperate pounding
To stay alive
It's all folly to try
For your relentless hold
Buries me alive

Skeletons

Skeletons—dry, rotting bones
In the earth is their home
Rotting in the sands of time
They're better off left alone
Not even one single bone
Is worth it to mine
Buried for all time
Is where they belong

Missing

I'm tired of being alone
I'm tired of being lonely
I miss the warmth of a man's embrace
I miss the feeling of a gentle kiss
I miss having someone to come home to
I miss having someone
Who cherishes my existence
I miss the joy of love

Mine

Defy me not!
Deny me not!
You will be mine,
And I will be yours.
For sure our love will grow,
As pure as the winter snow.

Hearts in Clouds

Hearts in clouds
Like hearts of lovers
Star crossed in the skies
Floating across the heavens
Drawn together by gentle breezes

My Love

His skin is as pale as porcelain
His hair as flaxen as a sheep's white wool
His eyes as blue as the summer sky
His smile as wide as the plains of Texas
His teeth so pretty and straight
His laugh as pleasant
As waves crashing on the beach
His embrace as warm as
A fire on a cold wintry night
His heart as generous and big
As the world itself
In his arms I lie so peaceful and calm
My troubles and fears washed away
By the great rivers of love
That pulse through my body and soul

Leeza Wilson

Without You

Without you my heart bleeds.
Without you my life is empty.
Without you my world is dark.
How long has it been
Since I've seen you?
The pain is no more
Only the emptiness remains.
My heart beats only for you.
But without you my heart will beat no more.

Valeriy

You were once my secret crush
Oh, how fond I was of you
I dreamed of walking hand in hand with you
Forever by your side, your one true adoring fan
But I was only a speck of dust in your eyes
A single soul in a sea of many
I watched you dance the ballet with such grace
So proud to boast that you were my friend
I wanted to call you mine
Oh, how I longed for that day
But my feelings for you I was too shy to say
And then you went your own way

My Slava

My Slava—my first love
My distant love
Held apart by land and sea
Your letters came frequently
Your words touched my heart
Your photos tantalized my eyes
Your calls, though rare,
Kept me from complete despair
I so patiently waited for the day
When "Will you marry me?" you would say
I longed to be with you forever
I dreamed of the day we would
Hand in hand walk through the wood
I dreamed of lying next to you,
Wrapped in the warmth of your embrace
But our distance was too great
Life would dole us another fate
And though our love was true and dear
We had to face our greatest fear
That together we would never be

Leeza Wilson

Poems by My Dad
David Knotts

God

As I think of God,
I feel stricken with awe,
When I read in his book,
I fear to break his law.
He tells us Him we should fear,
Because for us He truly cares.
Sometimes we make mistakes,
We may have committed some sin.
When we read in His book,
We find where others too have been.
He tells us in His book to pray to Him,
Ask forgiveness, and His favor we will win.
So never become downhearted and blue,
Because God forgives and really cares for you.

Sympathy

I am sorry about your loss,
That's the way it is
When through this life we waltz.
We think back of our good times,
We wonder sometimes how we got through,
And now have come the time
We are left lonely and blue.

Love

When you think of love,
What do you feel?
Do you think of caring, sharing, and giving?
Well, that's fine and good,
For it is part of living.
Can you think of words that are kind,
And look at another
And a better side you can find?
If your friend steps on your toe,
He or she is not really your foe.
Sometimes we hurt the one we're closest to;
This really makes them blue.
But just think,
What if it was just you?

Time

When you think of time, what do you feel?
If you're sick,
You think of the time when you will heal.
If you plan a trip,
You think of the time it will be,
You think of the time it will take.
You take time to make all of your plans,
In this way, you're sure to make no mistake.
Time is so endless and impossible to fake,
As it goes by we seem to just fade away.
But let's never give up hope,
As through the dark ages of time we grope.

David Knotts

Life

When you think of life,
Do you wonder how short it seems to be?
We work, we play,
And it seems to us
That in one place we always stay.
One day we realize though,
We have come a long way,
When we look in the mirror
And see our heads of gray.
As we look back to our younger days,
We might have received a lot of praise.
That might have been good
Or it could have been bad,
It depends upon how many people
You've made happy or sad.

Love Always

As the heavens from the earth
Is so far away,
By your side I always
Want to stay.
Broad and wide is the deep sea.
Your love, my dear, I always want to be.
I hope I can always
Make you happy.

A Dream

As I sit on the beach,
Playing in the sand,
In my mind's eye,
I can see a beautiful, distant land;
A land of stately trees and flowers,
A place I could spend many happy hours.
I see this land across the wide ocean.
I would like to be there now,
I have this notion.
They say all good things come to an end,
But all my good things just now begin.

David Knotts

My Love

As we walk hand in hand,
Determined that we will cross this hard land
We've had hard times
And we've had good times,
But happiness I hope we'll find in this rhyme.
As we walk and as we talk we grow in love
And I'm glad we do
Because I feel you've become my turtle dove.
You love me and I love you
And all our flowers will bloom in blue.
You are my flower,
You are my beautiful rose.
And the way I love you everyone will know
Because I'm sure it will show.
I love you with the deepest feeling,
And when I don't feel well,
And you are near
I can feel the healing.
When I'm with you
The sun will always shine
And my sky will always be blue.

Eternity

When we think of life in a hundred years,
We think of life without pain and tears.
When we think of life of a hundred years,
Why do some have of death such fears?
We live our lives to our best,
We'll live again if we have passed the test.
This we have as a promise sure,
Hopefully we have lived it just as pure.
We think of life forever more,
When we will not feel pain or see a sore.
This we have as a promise sure,
Provided we live and keep our senses pure.
It will be a great time to live and sing praise,
To the one who promises us this,
Let's not throw it amiss.
Living then will be beautiful in our eyes,
Because then we will be in Paradise.
There our eyes will always be blue
And flowers will always bloom.
We will have no fear
Because the wild beast and vicious animals
Will not in the brush loom.
When we think of forever
We think of singing praise
And this we will do with our voices raised.
This promise will not fail,
And to the One who promised
We will sing all Hail!

David Knotts

Just Me and My Grandson

Once I was young but now I've grown old.
Life would not be easy when I was young I was told.
I worked hard on the farm until twenty-one,
Then I worked hard at other things.
And now my work is enjoying my grandson.
At the end of the day, yes I'm tired,
But I lay back in my easy chair
And think of the things we've done,
Just me and my grandson.

I think he is the sweetest thing on earth,
And nothing in the world could buy his worth.
He is God's greatest gift to me.
He fills my life with so much joy and glee,
That's my grandson, just my grandson and me.
Together we do so many things,
Plant garden vegetables and pretty flowers.
Together in the yard we spend many happy hours.
We have so much fun,
Just me and my dear grandson.
No one can ever know how much I have won,
With the love between me
And my dear grandson.

Other Books by Leeza Wilson

Poetry Books

A Voice in the Wind

My Secret Garden and Other Poems for Children

Children's Non-fiction

My Grandpa is Extra Sweet—Diabetic Emergencies

The Germ Squad—Colds, Flu, and Stomach Bugs

Where is Your Heartbeat—Cardiac Emergencies (Coming soon)

About the Author

Leeza Wilson grew up with a fascination for notebooks and writing utensils. She began reading and writing at age four, mostly self-taught due to her independent and determined personality. She's had a love of books and reading her entire life which has fueled her love of writing. She writes stories that embrace the human psyche and relates the joys and struggles that we each face, and how we live through those moments. She writes in the genres of romance, mystery, suspense, historical, literary fiction, poetry, and children's.

When Leeza isn't writing, you can find her drawing and painting; spending time with her family; listening to music; volunteering with her local fire department; and playing the piano and guitar. She lives with her son, two cats, and Chihuahua in the Smoky Mountains of Tennessee.

Follow Leeza on Social Media

www.facebook.com/leezatheauthor

www.instagram.com/leezatheauthor

www.twitter.com/leezatheauthor

Get updates on new releases by Leeza Wilson and other authors at www.tsarinapress.com

Please Write a Review

Thank you for reading my book. It is my deepest wish that you had a pleasant reading experience and found my poems enjoyable. Whether you did or didn't, please feel free to get in touch and let me know what you thought. I love hearing from my readers and I always try my best to respond to emails from my fans. I value your honest feedback.

As any author will tell you, reviews are so very important in helping our books get noticed. I, like so many other authors, do not have a large marketing budget. Reviews help authors reach more readers by letting them know if a book is worth reading or not. So I rely a lot on reviews to help readers find my books and know if they're worthy of investing their time in to read. It only takes a couple of minutes to write a brief review of what you thought of the book. So if you can take a minute to write an honest review, I would greatly appreciate it, even if it's a negative review. All reviews matter, whether they're 1 star or 5 stars, a small essay or just one word.

Thank YOU

Leeza Wilson

www.ingramcontent.com/pod-product-compliance
Lightning Source LLC
Chambersburg PA
CBHW041959080526
44588CB00021B/2804